PERHAPS A MAN CAN
CHANGE THE STARS

ERIC'S PURSUIT OF PERPETUAL POTENTIAL

ROBERT L. STEARNS

ISBN-10 1439276986
EAN-13 9781439276983

FORWARD AND DEDICATION

I am writing this book in honor of my son Eric who died at the age of twenty one in April 2008. I am dedicating this book to my wife, Marianne, and my son Stephen, who have shown unbelievable strength, grace, and tenacity in trying to make good things happen in Eric's honor. I love you all with all of my heart.

The purpose of this book is to share with you three lessons that Eric's death taught me or reinforced for me. I remember reading stories and seeing movies about when a child dies in a family and what impact that has on the immediate family, extended family, and circle of friends. It has always been said that the death of a child is "the absolute worst thing that can happen to a parent." While Eric's death is the most painful experience of our lives, Marianne, Stephen, and I have made a decision to deal with this tragedy by consciously trying to make good things happen in Eric's memory. Furthermore, I am determined to use this experience to inspire people to perpetually pursue their personal potential, because you never know when it might be too late to accomplish something that you really want to accomplish.

Some of the good things that our family has done since Eric died include initiating two scholarships in his name.

One scholarship is awarded at his high school, North Allegheny, and one at his university, Penn State. Eric's goal in life was to do something that he would be remembered for. When he stated his goal at the beginning of the semester in Athens, it took the form of changing the way people do business in world markets. The scholarships are designed to help students do just that, and in the end to help Eric achieve his life's goal. I also speak to groups of students and share the three lessons I have learned in dealing with this tragedy with the hope that they will use these lessons to not only change the world, but to perpetually realize their full potential.

The next thing on our agenda of trying to make good things happen in Eric's name is to write this book. Our hopes are that this book will touch you and will inspire you to do everything that you can to achieve your innermost and fullest potential every day of your life. We sincerely hope that you will enjoy this book and hope that you will give us feedback about what these ideas have inspired you to do.

Sincerely,
Bob Stearns

PURPOSE

I am writing this book for several reasons:

- To honor my son Eric and to do something good in his name

- To inspire the readers to know that all people can strive to achieve their true potential and a more fulfilled life in spite of tragedy or any negative circumstances they are facing in their lives

- To try to combine the lessons I've learned in business and through Eric's death, which I hope readers will find of value

This third purpose is kind of tricky - trying to merge business concepts with a very personal story. The key theme that runs through both the personal and professional parts of my life is, I imagine, quite similar to many of your lives. As our lives evolve, we acquire different skills and talents. We apply some of these talents immediately, some dissipate, and some stay with us but remain dormant.

An important message which I hope you will take away from the book is that no matter what stage of life we are at, we all have the potential to explore. We have the potential to utilize and grow the talents and aspirations that we currently have. We have the potential to rekindle those talents that lie dormant and to allow new talents to blossom. Indeed, our Potential is Perpetual! This is true regardless of age, circumstances, and what other people may be telling us. So read, explore, and think deeply about whether you want to apply the three lessons I've learned from Eric. I sincerely hope that you do.

This is a book about triumph, tragedy, and the pursuit of true North. It is about triumph under positive circumstances and triumph over adversity. I don't want you to be sad when you are reading about what happened to Eric, but rather to rejoice in his life and what you can learn from it. Most of all I want you to accept Eric's challenge and go out there and "Change the Stars"!

My sincere thanks go out to everyone who was kind enough to read this book and offer suggestions. You have all truly added to the value of the book and helped to make the messages much clearer for the readers: Marianne Stearns, Stephen Stearns, Stefanie Manos, Jeanine Navarro, Christine Navarro, Katie Burt, Chuck Stern, Jason Gross, Jeff Tobe, Bonnie Budzowski, Linda Bishop, and Tony Pappis.

APRIL IN ATHENS

Midnight on Wednesday, April 16, 2008. I am sitting alone in my room in the Hilton in Athens writing thank you notes. Marianne flew home this morning to handle arrangements. Tomorrow I will accompany Eric back home. I have many people to thank for their kindness during the last twelve days. There is the wonderful group of people who run the Athens Centre: the owner, Rosemary, as well as Anthea, Nina, Dimitra, Vassia, and Katja. I also need to thank Ira, Kostas, Thomas, and Stavrina. Kees and the US Embassy staff. Jessica, Kurt, Phillip, and Diane. Bart and the Hilton Staff. Annie, Maria, Voula, and George from Delta. The students and citizens who donated blood… and many more who were strangers to us just twelve days and four thousand miles ago. Their capacity for kindness amazes me!

As I finish my notes, I see Eric's ginormous black suitcase against the wall opposite me. I am compelled to open the suitcase. Inside I find a portfolio with three poems that Eric had written when he was fifteen or sixteen years old. I'm not sure why he has those poems with him in Athens. I look at all of them, but one grabs me, it is titled "Stars."

I am remembering that moment of my life as I begin to write this book. I would like to share the ending of Eric's poem, which I first read that April night in Athens in 2008. His poem serves as both the title and the centerpiece for this book (the entire poem can be found at the end of the book).

Stars (fini) by Eric Michael Stearns

But some, some still fight, unable to accept, unable to deny, unable to ignore…Why? God's greatest gift to man… HOPE.

At the end of the day, Perhaps a man can change the stars.

Eric's poem gives you some insight into his character, and to his positive approach and outlook on life. I sincerely hope you discover some ways that you can "Change the Stars" in your life as you read this book.

I'm always with you, Dad…as I am always with you, my son!

THE BATTLEFIELDS OF GETTYSBURG

April 2, 2008 was a beautiful day. I was in Gettysburg, Pennsylvania speaking at a leadership conference. My presentation went very well, and I even had several people come up to me afterwards asking me to speak at their upcoming conferences. The conference ended in the early afternoon, and since I was in Gettysburg and had never been to visit the battlefields, I decided to take a ride over there. During the first day of the conference there was a screening of a film about the Civil War and I was thinking about that film as I was driving to the battlefields. Once I got there I spent a couple of hours exploring and roaming around, and towards the end of the afternoon I found myself at a battlefield called Little Round Top, which I remembered from the film.

The battle of Little Round Top took place on July 2, 1863. Of the 2,996 Union troops engaged, there were 565 casualties (134 killed, 402 wounded, 29 missing). The Confederacy losses were 1,185 out of 4,864 troops engaged. A total of 1,750 young men either lost their lives or were wounded that day. As I was looking over the battlefield, I could almost see those young men in my mind as I'd seen them the day before in the film at the conference. I remember thinking about the loss of life during this battle and how sad it must have been for their families.

What I didn't know at the time was that in almost exactly the same hour I was at Little Round Top and thinking about these boys, my own son Eric, who was four thousand miles away in Athens, Greece was about to lose his precious life.

So how was it that Eric was in Athens, Greece at the same time I was in Gettysburg? During the second semester of his junior year at Penn State, Eric had enrolled in a study abroad program in Athens from January of 2008 through the end of April, 2008. He was about three weeks away from coming home when he was killed.

I had about a four-and-a-half-hour ride back from Gettysburg to my home just north of Pittsburgh, Pennsylvania, and I was feeling content on this ride home. The conference had gone well, Eric was going to be coming home soon, my son Stephen was finishing his first year in college and doing well, and Marianne and I were truly enjoying life. I got home about eight o'clock, and then as I was getting settled, the phone rang.

It was the woman from Penn State who had coordinated the semester abroad program. "Mr. Stearns," she said, "I'm calling to let you know that your son Eric has been in an accident in Athens, and he's in surgery right now." I literally couldn't believe what I was hearing, and as she told me more of the details, this feeling of disbelief magnified into horror.

She gave me the name of the leader of the program in Athens, a woman named Rosemary. I called her immediately. Rosemary told me that Eric had been through one surgery already and that they couldn't stop the bleeding in the femoral artery in his leg. They were trying to arrange a second surgery for Eric.

Somehow I was able to take my focus off Eric's injury for a moment, and I asked her what happened. She told me that Eric and a friend had been walking on the sidewalk and that a driver had lost control of his car and driven up on the sidewalk. The car hit Eric and grazed the friend he was walking with. I asked Rosemary to keep in touch with me and let me know as soon as Eric got through the second surgery. Marianne was at a community meeting and I had to call the police to get her out of it. I didn't want to relay the horrible news about what happened to Eric to her over the telephone, but I had no choice. The police asked her if she wanted them to escort her, but she insisted on driving herself home. While Marianne was driving home, I went online and looked for the first flight that we could take to Athens. It wasn't until ten o'clock the next morning.

ERIC MICHAEL STEARNS

Eric Michael Stearns was born on January 17, 1987 to two very proud parents. My wife, Marianne, and I had gotten married in 1980, and we'd been trying to have a child for several years without much success. In 1986 I accepted an assignment to run three condominium hotels in Myrtle Beach, South Carolina. It was during our time there that Marianne became pregnant, and we were thrilled! Our son Stephen was born about a year and a half later, and then our family was complete.

Eric was a regular boy with one exception, he was born with size fourteen feet. I swear it's true, or at least it seemed that way (his aunt says he got them from me). He was a deep thinker, a dreamer, and he was filled with wanderlust. I remember when Eric was no more than two years old; we took him to the zoo with my sister and her boyfriend. We turned to look at the elephants for less than a minute, and when we turned back, Eric was gone. Of course we panicked and started looking all over the grounds of the zoo, and finally we found him.

Eric did this sort of thing all the time. A couple of examples will serve to demonstrate this. One summer we took a beach vacation to the Jersey shore. It was getting towards dusk, and Eric, who was fourteen at the time, decided he was going to run the boardwalk. I waited and waited and waited for him to come back, but no Eric. It was getting dark, so I finally decided to try to find him, and I started to jog down the boardwalk. Sure enough, after what seemed like an eternity, I found Eric. It was just about pitch black, and he was just walking at a leisurely pace towards me, and he seemed to think nothing of it. He was "just exploring."

Another example took place at Hilton Head beach. The whole family went bike riding, and once again Eric decided to venture off on his own path. Once again we couldn't find him, so finally I got in the car and started to drive all over the place. Again after what seemed like a very long time, there was Eric walking back toward us with his bicycle, flat tire and all.

Eric was also a dreamer and he loved to write. As a matter of fact he even wrote a book. He created characters that were so well developed it was as if he knew them like friends. I always wondered how he came up with them. He dreamed of being an author, and this was a source of some conflict for Eric because he also wanted to become a businessman. He wasn't sure how he could do both, and he struggled with this for years, finally resolving it during his trip to Greece.

Eric was a deep thinker. He would try to think of all angles of just about everything; this was both a blessing and a curse. It was a blessing because he was able to see things that other people didn't necessarily see. He was able to listen to people and to watch their body language, and from doing this he could ascertain what was really going on in the other person's mind. He was also able to predict things that could happen in many different situations by thinking through the possibilities and scenarios that might take place. It was a curse because he would sometimes read meanings into situations that just were not there.

Eric (far right) had the ability to make __anyone__ feel a part of the group.

FROM SIBLING RIVALRY
TO BROTHERHOOD:
STEPHEN'S RECOLLECTIONS OF ERIC

One of Stephen's memories of Eric starts with them both arriving home from high school. My office is at home and pretty close to the front door, so I heard them come in and was ready to greet them. The next thing I heard was no less than an all out barroom brawl in our front entryway. I had to jump in between them so they wouldn't hurt each other. Well I succeeded in doing that, but I didn't arrive early enough to prevent them from breaking the banister to the stairs leading to the second floor of the house. I separated them with a few choice words and exacted a promise from them to pay for the damage (I don't think I ever saw the cash).

As Stephen recently recalled this incident for me, I asked him why it happened. He told me that every day when they got home from school, Eric made Stephen dig in his backpack to get the front door key. Eric would never dig into his backpack to get his own key. Stephen finally got tired of it and they argued, which led to the scuffle in our front entryway. This rivalry faded away into a true love and friendship as they got older. They affectionately referred to each other as "Bro" and became the best of friends. This is something that I had secretly wished would happen and that their relationship would always remain close as they grew up together.

I asked Stephen what qualities he truly admired in Eric. He listed these: first, his creativity, his ability to think of stories and solutions that others wouldn't necessarily come up with; second, his ability to influence people and circumstances; and third, his intelligent thinking. Eric was always one step ahead and knew what was coming next. I also asked Stephen what he most learned from Eric. He said, "Never to settle for second best. Eric always wanted to be the best at everything he did. He had a passion for life and always tried to achieve the best possible outcome in everything he did."

When Eric was a junior in high school he announced to us that he was going to go to college in California, which was at the other end of the country from where we live. Why did he want to go to California? So he could travel and see different places; the school he attended was secondary. We wanted him closer to home so we could easily visit him and he could easily come home. So we told him that he could go anywhere he wanted to as long as he was no more than four hours away from our home in Pittsburgh. That is how Eric ended up going to Penn State University, or at least one of the reasons why he went there. Eric had expressed this deep need to travel to us even earlier. When he was in the fifth grade he told us that he wanted to go to Greece which was the home country of my wife and her family. It was because of this burning desire to go to Greece that we agreed to let him take that trip in his junior year at Penn State.

SPEND A SUMMER DAY:
ERIC CHOOSES HIS ALMA MATER

Towards the end of his junior year, Eric, Marianne, and I decided to visit several universities so Eric could decide where he wanted to go to school. Eric was an excellent student and was consistently on the honor roll. He also won a Pennsylvania statewide award for entrepreneurship when he was in high school. His academic excellence carried over to Penn State, where he made the Dean's list each year. But how did Eric end up at Penn State?

Since we wouldn't support his desire to go to California for school, Eric somehow locked on to attending a small college in eastern Ohio. Eric and his friend Andy met a recruiter from that school at a college fair, and this recruiter did a good job of selling the school to both of them. We agreed to visit the school, as long as Eric would also take a look at Penn State. We visited the school in Ohio, but Marianne and I weren't thrilled with it, which of course made it all that more appealing to Eric. As we left Ohio for Penn State, Eric sat in the back seat of the car moaning, "I don't know why we're going to Penn State; I'm not going to enroll there. I want to go to school in Ohio." This went on for the full four-hour car ride. No matter how much we tried to reason with him, Eric wouldn't relent.

We finally arrived at the Nittany Lion Inn, an old English style hotel with a wonderful mix of new and old amenities and ambiance. We went to dinner in the hotel dining room, and Eric continued his lament. "There's no way I'm going to Penn State, let's just go home." We had registered to attend a Penn State event the next day, which was called "Spend a Summer's Day at Penn State." The event was designed to allow prospective students to learn about the college through some structured events and some unstructured time for them to explore the campus. We attended the opening event, which was hosted by the recruiting office. The speaker did an excellent job of describing the Penn State experience without making a blatant sales pitch.

Next we wandered around campus and visited the English Literature department. Eric got a chance to talk with several people about how he could advance his writing interests. Then we went to Smeal Business College, where Eric got to talk with several people about the school's business offerings. As we left Smeal, one of the professors grabbed us completely unsolicited and asked, "Have you seen the stock market trading room?" We had not, so she escorted us to a room that was a facsimile of a New York Stock Exchange trading room. Penn State was the first University, or one of the first, to install this type of room on their campus.

As we left the stock trading room and said thank you to the professor, Eric turned to Marianne and me and said, "I'm going to Penn State!", and that was that. We were/are really pleased with the professionalism and hospitality that the school has provided, so much so that we encouraged Stephen to also attend that university, and he gladly did. Eric had a great tenure at Penn State, both academically and socially.

Eric was a fun-loving kid who oftentimes took the lead in organizing different events for his friends. We found out from his friends that Eric was also the social director among his friends at the college. Whenever his friends were looking for something to do, the first phone call went to Eric who put all the plans and gatherings together. Eric also assumed this role with his classmates in Athens. We were told that he was the driving force in keeping a group of twenty-three students from different parts of the country and different schools together. After Eric died, I asked his friends if they would write about how they remembered Eric. Their stories will give you some insights about Eric and how he influenced the lives of others.

ERIC: ALWAYS REACHING OUT
BY NORA HENNICK

I guess the most striking thing about Eric during our time in Greece was his constant reaching out to others. For the most part, we were an extremely close group, but about halfway through the semester, as is bound to happen, groups had formed, and two girls in particular found themselves excluded. We all noticed this and had sort of given up making the extra effort to include them, but Eric consistently made an effort to include them and spend time with them. I know seeing Eric reach out made the rest of us renew our efforts as well. Most of my best memories of Eric are simple - lighthearted banter or more serious conversations about religion or our futures. He was always a thoughtful, interesting conversation partner, an exceptional listener. I feel very lucky to have known him, and I miss him so very much.

Eric's classmates at the Athens Centre

EARLY MEMORIES BY JASON BARASH
(A FRIEND OF ERIC'S FROM AGE SIX)

My earliest memories with Eric are from when he first moved into our neighborhood; I was so excited when I heard there was another boy my age coming into Brook Park. Being on the same baseball team was one thing, but the thing that really made me appreciate the type of person he was started on the bus rides every morning to McKnight Elementary. On that short fifteen-minute ride, I laughed the whole time and forgot where I was going. He would bring in little toys and put on shows for me every morning. His sense of humor was unique, unlike any other boy of that age. Growing up, I was the shy kid of the group, but being around him gave me courage to do new things and not really care about what people thought. That's how he was. He was going to give things a try and not take no for an answer. Eric was truly unique; there was never a dull moment when I was around him. Thank you from the bottom of my heart for bringing Eric into my life. He has left a mark on me that will last forever.

IT IS FITTING
BY CAMERON MILLER

I think that it is fitting that Penn State University is going to permanently honor Eric with a collage in the business school because he left a lasting impression with everyone who ever had the pleasure of meeting him. I will never forget Eric and will miss him for the rest of my life.

These three stories give you a little insight into Eric's character. I'll share more stories from his friends throughout this book.

THE FLIGHT TO SAVE ERIC

During our flight from Pittsburgh to New York, Eric was still in the operating room. We found out later that Eric had lost thirty pints of blood due to the severing of his femoral artery. The surgery that he had while we were on the flight was a final attempt to stop the bleeding. When we landed in New York, I called Rosemary, and she told us that there was still no result from surgery, so we got on the plane from New York to Athens not knowing if Eric was going to survive. The first person I saw when we got on that plane was a flight attendant named Annie. I explained the situation to Annie and asked her to please let me know if any messages came through on the radio of the plane about Eric, which she agreed to do. As I settled into my seat, the words "Don't quit" kept running through my mind as I thought about Eric alone in an operating room four thousand miles away from home.

The next thing we knew, every member of the flight crew was stopping back to check on us and make sure we were as comfortable as we could be under the circumstances. This was a kind and wonderful thing for Annie to do. What we didn't know at the time was that this was to be the beginning of a longstanding relationship with

Annie, who was a complete stranger only moments before I walked onto the plane.

Annie came to the hospital to visit Eric and she had several meals with us while she was in Athens. Annie and her husband came to Eric's funeral and she has kept in touch with us to this day. This was the second example of a spiritual event that occurred as a result of Eric being struck by a reckless driver; a complete stranger had become a fast friend to us. The first spiritual event was the fact that Eric was struck by the car at the same time I was thinking about the poor young men who lost their lives during the battle of the Round Top as part of America's Civil War.

The next thing I remember was being in a taxicab with Rosemary from the Athens Centre, where Eric had been attending school. The school's taxi driver, George, was driving us from the airport to the hospital in Athens, Greece. I kept saying in my head to Eric, "Don't quit."

THE HOSPITAL

Rosemary suggested that we check in at the hotel before going to the hospital. We did this quickly and then walked briskly to the hospital, which was only a ten-minute walk from the hotel. The Evangelismos Hospital had been built in the early 1900s and was old and not in very good shape. Rosemary explained that hospitals in Athens rotate each day in terms of which ones will accept emergency cases. The night that Eric was struck by the car, this particular hospital, which was operated by the Greek government, was the one where emergency cases were taken. Because of travel time, it was now April 4, almost two days after Eric had been hit by a car.

We arrived in the ICU at the hospital and asked to see Eric. Of course no one at the hospital could speak English, so we relied on Rosemary to be our eyes, ears, nose, hands, and feet. She and the team at the Athens Centre fulfilled this role for us for the next two weeks. The staff at the hospital would not allow us in to see Eric as they had strict rules that visiting hours were only one time each day. We had traveled over four thousand miles, over a day and a half, and they wouldn't let us see our son—I was angry! Rosemary pleaded with them, and finally they let us go and see Eric. It was then that I realized that Marianne and I

would have very little control over the events that were to
unfold from this point forward.

When I first saw Eric, he was one of sixteen people lying
on individual beds in the same intensive care unit. His face
was visible, but they had the sheets pulled tightly to his
chest, so it was impossible to tell what other type of injuries he had. His whole body was swollen from the fluids
they had pumped into him to try to keep him stable, and
he was on a ventilator to help him breathe. He was uncon-
scious and sedated, but as soon as I started talking to him
his eyes started to flutter as if he recognized my voice. I
stayed with him for a while, and then Marianne went in to
see him. She told me afterwards that when she talked to
him, she saw a tear come to the corner of his eye as if he
recognized her.

We talked to the doctor afterwards, and he told us that
Eric's legs were severely damaged, and he had lost a lot
of blood. In essence the original complement of blood in
his body had to be fully replaced. They told us that they
had asked for blood donations and that there were stories
in the local newspapers as well as television stations asking for people to donate blood. The outpouring of people who donated blood was amazing. The people at the
hospital said they'd never seen so much blood donated
for a patient for as long as the hospital had been in existence. This is a true tribute to the Greek people, to the other

American students in Athens, and to the US Embassy in Greece.

We were with Eric every day, but unfortunately there was not much progress.

We did get a little bit of positive news on April 7, but the day after that, on April 8, 2008, we lost our beautiful son Eric.

The next thing that I had to do was to call my son Stephen back home at Penn State to tell him what had happened. This was as hard for me to do as seeing Eric lying lifeless in the hospital bed had been. I spoke to Stephen first, and then Marianne talked to him. He was devastated but exceptionally brave. I felt terrible that I could not be with him in person, but at the same time I knew that Stephen would be OK until we got home because of his inner strength and faith in God. Fortunately my sister-in-law and brother-in-law were with him and drove him from school to our home.

*Eric in Meteora in Northern Greece, Perhaps God had a
higher purpose for him*

A Higher Purpose

The day after Eric died, Rosemary invited Marianne and me to come to her home to greet Eric's teachers and fellow students, some of whom we had already met. This was very kind of Rosemary, and we agreed to join them. During the afternoon before we went to Rosemary's, we sat outside drinking coffee at a Greek Taverna. I remember a strange thought coming into my mind: "I'm sure there will be other people who experience this type of tragedy and loss in their lives in the future. Whenever I'm ready, I would like to help these people." Why was I thinking this when I should have been just feeling sad about losing Eric? To this day I'll never know. Perhaps this was the beginning of God allowing me to deal with Eric's death in a positive light instead of letting sadness consume me. What I didn't know as I was thinking this was that more spiritual occurrences were about to happen.

We arrived at Rosemary's home around seven o'clock that evening. Many of the students whom we had met earlier when they visited Eric in the hospital were already there, as were some of the teachers. They greeted us individually and were very kind to us. About one hour passed and then one of Eric's classmates, Lindsey, brought out her laptop computer and asked us if she could show us something.

We proceeded to watch as on the screen appeared picture after picture of Eric. His fellow students had taken pictures with him at various locations around Greece that they had visited during the semester. The pictures had been put to music and were choreographed such that it looked like a professional movie. The video lasted about twenty minutes, and tears were flowing freely from my eyes as I watched the pictures flash on the screen. At first I was very sad, but the sadness quickly turned into a revelation that Marianne and I would always have this beautiful memory of Eric. It certainly was not and would never be the same as having Eric with us, but at least we would have these memories, and we would see a little bit of what Eric saw while he was in Greece.

At the end of the video I turned to a young woman by the name of Katja, who was one of the staff members at the Athens Centre, and said to her, "He was a beautiful young man, and it's a shame that he will never reach his fullest potential."

Katja, without blinking, said to me, "No, Bob, you're wrong. Eric has achieved his potential here on this earth. Now he will go on to achieve even greater things in the next universe." I remember that I got very angry with Katja because of what she said, but after a couple of days my anger turned to something else. I began to feel that what Katja said to me could possibly be true.

After my brief conversation with Katja, I asked Rosemary and the students if they would mind if I said a few words. Marianne and I both knew that everyone in the room was feeling sad for us, and I didn't want them to feel that way. Furthermore they had all had such a wonderful three-month journey including cultural and architectural discovery in Greece as well as personal discovery.

I didn't want Eric's death to overshadow the wonderful experience that they had enjoyed. So I just started talking from the heart. There were two key lessons that I talked about. First, *Never quit*. The Greek words for this are, "Min ta Paratas." Second, *Focus on what you do have, not on what you don't have*. I must have talked for about half an hour, but it seemed much longer. I could see that my words were having a calming effect on everybody in the room, which was what I had intended. When I finished talking, the students applauded, which surprised me.

The video that the students made became a lighthouse in the wilderness for the hundreds of people who streamed in to visit and console us at the funeral home. Marianne, Stephen, and I found ourselves in the reverse role of consolers to many of those who came to see us. Whenever people were particularly sad, I would take them into the parlor and ask them to watch the video. "Do you see the look on Eric's face in these pictures?" I would say. "Do you see how happy he is? How many people can say that they died doing exactly what they wanted to do?" I continued. The exhilarating pictures of Eric had an immediate calming effect upon everyone who viewed them.

It made me immediately think, "Why is it that I am feeling the need to comfort them with my words? How did I have the strength to put these thoughts together tonight after my son had died?" It was eerily similar to the thoughts I'd had in the afternoon about wanting to help other people who have gone through a similar experience. Why was it that God was giving me the strength to speak and was pointing me in this direction? Perhaps it was a coping mechanism, perhaps it was an outlet for my emotions, perhaps it was just cathartic...or perhaps there was a higher purpose beginning to be revealed to me.

Over the years that have passed since we lost Eric, I have tried to make sense of what happened. I realize that only God knows why Eric was taken at the prime of his life, but I have been driven to try to make something good come from his death. My life's work has been devoted to helping organizations to achieve their fullest potential. When Eric died, my thoughts and focus widened to thinking about how individuals could achieve their fullest potential regardless of their current circumstances. My thought process has expanded so that I now believe that all of us have what I'll call Perpetual Potential™. The rest of this book is devoted to the three lessons I've learned, that will enable you to pursue Perpetual Potential.

What is Perpetual Potential ™? Is it Really Possible?

Perpetual Potential: Hidden, forgotten, or latent talent that we can develop if we so choose. Furthermore, these talents or skills may be things that we always wanted to achieve but for one reason or another never pursued.

The first two keys to pursuing Perpetual Potential:

- Never quit.
- Focus on what you do have, not on what you don't have.

***Eric celebrates his 21st birthday on
the beautiful island of Santorini***

THE THREE LESSONS ABOUT PERPETUAL POTENTIAL BECOME A LITTLE CLEARER

This story goes back to our time in Athens. The higher purpose that I mentioned earlier started to become clearer about a week after we met with Eric's classmates at Rosemary's house. Marianne had returned home from Greece a day earlier than me to take care of arrangements. The night before I was scheduled to return home with Eric, I was looking through some of his belongings, and I found those three poems that he had written back when he was fifteen or sixteen years old. I don't know why he had these poems with him on his trip to Greece, but I remembered him telling me about a poetry course that he took during his sophomore year of high school. I couldn't get the poem "Stars" out of my mind.

Over five hundred people attended Eric's funeral, and I felt compelled to speak to them after the service. I did this for three reasons. Primarily I wanted to honor Eric and celebrate his life; secondly I knew that everybody who was there felt badly for us, and I wanted to try to lift their spirits. The third reason, quite honestly, is that it always makes me feel good to speak about Eric.

I spoke about the same two lessons that I spoke to the students in Athens about never quitting and focusing on what you do have not on what you don't have. This time I added a third lesson: "Change the Stars," and I read Eric's poem to the people assembled at his funeral. Immediately as the poem ended, the people at the funeral began to applaud. Afterwards, as people greeted Marianne, Stephen, and me, I was very surprised but very happy to hear from them that they had felt uplifted by the three lessons that I shared with them. It was at that moment that I realized what a powerful message I had been given in the face of this tragedy. I would like to share how this message has evolved for me and how I believe that it can be helpful to you as you seek to perpetually reach your personal potential. As I continue to think about and evolve the three lessons I am about to share with you, they take on an even deeper meaning for me.

LESSON NUMBER ONE: TACKLE TOUGH CHALLENGES AND NEVER QUIT

As I mentioned earlier, Eric was born with size fourteen feet. The first time I saw him tackle a tough challenge was when he was about eight years old on the baseball field. He got a late start playing baseball compared to the other kids, but somehow his coach decided to play him as the catcher. I was very proud of Eric as he donned his chest protector and catcher's mask, as that was the position I had played when I was a kid. The team's best pitcher, a fastballer named Josh, was on the pitcher's rubber (the kids were too young for a true pitcher's mound). Every time Josh threw a pitch, Eric couldn't seem to get his feet out of the way, and his toes got stung, but he hung in there anyway. Josh is now a major league pitcher.

The first time I saw my son Stephen tackle a tough challenge was also on the baseball field. He was playing left field and a long fly ball came out to him. There was a runner on third tagging up to score. Stephen had to quickly track the ball down and his throw to the catcher had to be a strike. Stephen took the challenge and threw the runner out.

*Eric (on the left) in the Greek Olympic Stadium,
home to the ancient Gladiators.
His much bigger friend Matt is a tough
challenge, but Eric persists and doesn't quit!*

Staying with sports stories, Eric also exhibited the "never quit" attitude on the basketball court. He decided to try his hand at this sport, and he made the seventh grade team even though he wasn't one of the better players. He was a hard worker, however, and his coach recognized that. Slowly Mr. Miller let him play in some of the games. One of the highlights for Eric that first year on the team in seventh grade was when he competed in a shooting contest. Eric was the first person to sink a shot from half court, and for those efforts he won a football that was autographed by the Pittsburgh Steelers. He gave the ball to Marianne, who is an avid Steelers fan, and she loved it.

One of the skills that Eric worked on during his basketball practices was the ability to make a left-handed layup. He became quite proficient at lefty layups, and as a matter of fact, he became the best at this skill on the team. This "niche" skill that he developed further enhanced his standing with his coach. In eighth grade, Eric became a platoon player along with his friend Ryan. Pretty soon he was playing about one third of every game. Then a breakthrough occurred. About halfway through the season, Eric started his first game and remained a starter for most of the rest of the season. Eric was playing over half of the minutes in the game, which made him feel really good and confident and confirmed to him the value of the Tackle Tough Challenges and Never Quit mentality. This mentality stuck with him for the rest of his life.

When Marianne and I were on our way over to Greece, and I was exhorting Eric, "Don't quit," in my thoughts, I had no idea how tough the challenge was that he was facing due to the injuries he sustained from the car that struck him. Our bodies typically contain about ten pints of blood, so Eric had lost the full complement of blood in his body three times over after the car hit him and as we were traveling to try to see and save him. Despite that, Eric didn't quit; he stayed alive so that we could see him.

STEPHEN

Stephen perhaps had the most difficult challenge in dealing with Eric's death. You see, he was back in college in the States, and while Marianne and I could see what was happening, he really couldn't. We decided to try to communicate as much positive information on Eric's condition to Stephen over the telephone as we could to try to keep Stephen's spirits up as well. When Eric died, I had to tell Stephen about this over the phone from four thousand miles away. It took about ten days for us to take care of Eric's affairs in Greece before we could come home, so Stephen was basically dealing with this without his parents for that length of time.

About a month after Eric's death, Stephen had to take final exams at Penn State. He came through his finals quite well. I honestly don't know if I could have been as strong. Stephen could have quit right then and there, and I don't know whether I could have blamed him for that. His inner strength even at such a young age allowed him to carry on. That spirit of perseverance has served him well ever since.

MARIANNE

I think a child's death affects his or her mother most strongly. After all, Marianne was responsible for the bulk of nurturing Eric as he grew up, as most mothers are. Marianne has talked to many people who have sought her out over the last couple of years to find out how she has had the strength and courage to deal with Eric's death. In addition to dealing with Eric's death, Marianne was the president of her church at that time. She could have very easily given up that role, and everybody would have understood. However, she knew the church was going through some difficult transitions so she decided to stick it out and was very successful in helping the members of the church to come back together in friendship and to increase attendance at weekly church services. I honestly don't know how she did it, but once again I think it points to the inner strength that she has. We all have this inner strength to varying degrees. This strength and the Never Quit mentality allows us to tackle tough challenges and keep going, to explore new possibilities, and to achieve much more than most of us believe we can achieve.

I'd now like to share with you quotes from some people you might have heard of about tackling tough challenges and never quitting:

Winston Churchill on Never Quitting

"Never give in. Never give in. Never, never, never, never—in nothing great or small, large or petty—never give in except to convictions of honor and good sense."

Ross Perot on Never Quitting

"Most people give up just when they are about to achieve success. They quit on the one-yard line. They give up at the last minute of the game, three feet from winning."

BOB

I'd like to share with you a couple of personal stories where I didn't quit in terms of seeking and achieving my Perpetual Potential. The first one oddly enough also starts on the baseball field for me when I was a kid. I was a fat little kid and not a very good athlete, and therefore my Little League career was not very good. I was fortunate to have a friend named Barry who tried to help me to get better. He did this by constantly working with me one-on-one on the baseball diamond and also by challenging me to become more physically fit. When I was thirteen years old, he introduced me to a really good coach, Steve, who decided to take a chance on me. Steve turned me into a catcher (much like my son Eric). At first I was not very good, but the coach stuck with me, and I practiced constantly. Long story short,

I became pretty good and was the starting catcher on my high school team as well as the American Legion team. This was very important in developing my personal belief about never quitting.

Fast-forward many years to the day I decided to start my own consulting business in 1985. I started the business basically just because I wanted to and really didn't know what I was getting into. The roots of deciding to start the business go back to my father, Eli. My dad only finished the eighth grade in school and then had to go to work to help support his family. When he was old enough, he enlisted in the Navy and fought in World War II. When he got back to the States, he became a salesman in the home construction business and eventually opened his own business, which he called Beechwood Homes. I worked for my Dad as a salesman during a couple of summers while I was in high school as a salesman. My job was to "cold call", knock on people's doors and convince them to bring my father in to close the sale. I really hated doing that, but it was great basic training in selling, which has served me well in my career.

The seeds for being an entrepreneur, running my own business, and being my own boss were sown during those summers, and in 1985 those seeds bore flowers. Still, I didn't really understand how difficult of a challenge I had undertaken in opening my business. In 1991 I found myself with lots of clients but not making a lot of money. One of those clients asked me to come to work for them, and after some painful soul searching, I decided to accept their offer. I accepted the offer only after negotiating to continue to operate my consulting business on a part time basis. I always knew in my heart and mind that some-day I would go back 100 percent into my own business. Ten years later in 2000, that's exactly what I did, and for-tunately the business has been very good to me and my family since that time.

Never Quit when you start up a New Venture

When I first started my business in 1985, I really didn't understand all of the challenges that were in front of me. I had been told that most new businesses failed in the first 5 years, but I decided to take on the challenge anyway. In 1991, I went to running my busi-ness part time. I always knew I would go back to run-ning it full time, and in 2000, I did! Now I had a much more valuable set of skills to offer to my clients.

What new business start up idea have
you been thinking about launching?
When is the right time? Perhaps the time is now!

Interestingly enough, while I was working with this client between 1991 and 2000, I learned another lesson in "tackling tough challenges and never quitting." During my first three years with the company, I was involved in Organizational Development and Process Improvement. During those years I led employee teams who were responsible for saving fifty million dollars for the company.

Despite those great results, I felt we could do better, so I approached the CEO and told him so. He said, "Bob, if you can find something better, bring it to me, and we'll give it a try." What I brought back to Tom was something called the Malcolm Baldrige Award, which is the most demanding system for Business Excellence in the country. Every year, the President of the United States gives this award to companies that excel in leadership, strategic planning, customer loyalty, information and performance measurement, employee engagement, process improvement, and business results. Baldridge recipients typically achieve results that outperform the stock market. Over the next six years, I led the efforts at the company to implement the Baldridge process. The company won the Baldridge award in 2003.

However, not everybody in the company was happy when we started our Baldridge journey. Quite the opposite, only the CEO, the vice president of operations, and I were really enthusiastic about following the Baldridge criteria. I remember quite clearly what the CEO said to me when we started this process. "Bob, you are responsible for implementing the Baldridge process, but you can't use me as a club to force people to adopt these practices and criteria. Instead, your job is to convince all nine hundred people in the company that this is a good thing for them as individuals and for the company as a whole." During those six years when I was implementing Baldridge, many times I felt like I was banging my head against the wall, and many times I felt like I should quit. What kept me going was the very strong belief that Baldridge was good for a company as well as for all of the people in the company.

Many of the other members of the senior leadership team openly fought me as I tried to implement Baldrige. One vivid memory comes from a monthly meeting that we held called the Quality Forum. The purpose of the forum was to introduce new concepts to the company leaders at all levels of the company. I can remember presenting some information about Baldridge when the Vice President of Marketing, who was the number two person at the company, stood up and challenged me. "Bob, what makes you think that we are even interested in going for the Baldridge award? We're already a pretty good company. After all, we have a large share of the market. We have high ratings from our customers and high ratings from our employees. I believe you are being very presumptuous to think that we're even interested in going after Baldridge."

<u>Can one person change the Culture
and Results of a whole company?</u>

I had an idea. The idea was that the Baldrige Process could dramatically improve both the culture of my company, and the business results that my company achieved. I found a way (actually many ways) to influence 900 other people that Baldrige would be beneficial to the company and to them individually. This company has now won the Baldrige Award (the Super Bowl of Business) twice.

What are your ideas to change the
culture and results in your company?
Is it important enough for you to find a way
to influence the change? I bet it is!
It takes just one person with a good idea
to change the way business is done.
Who is the first person you need to influence?

Well I dealt with that comment at the forum, but I can tell you that his words set our Baldridge efforts back quite a bit.

Something else that I learned on this particular journey was that it was very important to align the goals of the Baldridge process with the operational and business goals of the company in order for the company to achieve its potential. This is the foundation of a high performance company. For the first year of trying to implement this process, I did not have those goals in alignment. What happened was that people treated the Baldridge process as an aside, something that they would do when time allowed. The second year I got a little smarter. During the goal setting process for our senior leadership team, I included the goals for implementing Baldridge. This alignment of goals from top to bottom in an organization is a key element of the Baldridge philosophy and made it a lot easier to get people to pay attention to this initiative.

Another member of our senior leadership team also fought the implementation of Baldridge very openly. He was the CFO. I remember having several meetings with him to try to get him on board, and we could never see eye to eye. Finally one day I met with him, and at the end of the meeting he looked at me and said, "Bob I may not agree with your ideas and methods, but I do have to tell you, I admire you for your tenacity. You do the same thing that I do when you can't get people to understand and buy into what you're saying with one approach. You come back around again and try another approach. That is the reason why even though I won't fully buy into what you're telling me, I will indeed try to work with you as you are implementing this new Baldridge philosophy."

These two gentlemen eventually became the company's top two senior leaders, and when the company won the Baldridge Award in 2003, they were the first two people to identify themselves as champions of the Baldridge process. I found this both interesting and amusing, but was really happy that they had both come around to realize the value of this process. I often think that if I had quit, if I had let the naysayers win the battle, if I hadn't been the driving force behind the Baldridge process, what a negative impact that would have had on the company, and frankly what an opportunity I would have missed.

> It is possible to change even the greatest doubters into believers. Ask yourself, what haven't I yet tried to influence their opinion? Remember that data defies disbelief, and don't quit!

You see I learned so much during those six years that it enabled me to go back full time to my consulting practice and to help countless other organizations. I do want to share a very positive story with you that occurred during the Baldridge journey. I walked into one of the departments at the company one day. They made a product called a "connector tube." I asked them what was the biggest problem they were having in their department. They told me that the biggest problem they had was something called a "kinked connector tube."

What would happen is that a tube would become bent in half and would no longer allow air or liquid to pass through it and had to be thrown away. I asked them how many of these kinked connector tubes they had every month, and they told me that it was four hundred. I then asked him how long this has been going on, and they said, "Oh, 'bout ten years."

I asked what they had done about it, and they told me that they had talked with some engineers a couple of years ago but never got a response back. Then I asked them the magic question: "What do you think is the problem?"

They said, "Bob, we think that when people are hired, they are just thrown into the job without any training and never learn how to do the job right, and therefore they end up making a lot of kinked connector tubes." This was the magic question because the people that work closest to the job know best what the problems and what the solutions are. It is the leader's role to create the environment where people feel comfortable bringing up problems and then give them the time, training, and tools to solve them.

During the next couple of weeks I asked the employees of that department to train me how to make these connector tubes. This was done in a clean room environment, so I was dressed in a lab coat, a bonnet hair covering, and booties. As they trained me they wrote a training manual.

I had nothing to do with writing this manual. When the manual was finished, they implemented a training program with their fellow employees, and within thirty days the number of kinked connector tubes dropped from four hundred a month to one hundred a month. Can you imagine, this was a problem that had gone on for ten years and within six to eight weeks they had fixed 75 percent of the problem. Well, I was feeling pretty good about this; as a matter of fact I was getting ready to celebrate with members of that department when a young man named John started waving his arms. John worked in the department and was sitting in the back of the room. He said with a firm voice, "Bob, we can't celebrate yet. We still have a hundred kinked connector tubes every month, and I've got the solution."

John reached into his pocket and pulled out one of these large pencil erasers and showed me that he had hollowed out part of the eraser with a penknife. He said, "I believe what is causing the rest of the problem is the clip we are using when we are making the connector tubes, and I developed a model of the clip that I think will solve the problem completely." We gave John's model to the engineers, who built the clip, and once the clip was utilized…*Zero* kinked connector tubes. To give you an order of magnitude of the solution these employees developed, over the years this one improvement has saved that company millions of dollars. There are many lessons to be taken from this story. This is just one example of the many fruits the Baldridge process yielded.

<u>A Company can only Fulfill its Potential when all Employees Fulfill Theirs</u>

1) All I did with the connector department is ask them what they thought the problem was; this is the magic question.

2) The people who work closest to the job know best what the problems and solutions are. The Leader's role is to create the culture and environment where employees can fulfill their potential.

3) Never quit, you might just make millions!

What can you do to enable your employees to fulfill their potential, so that your company can fulfill its potential?

My leadership of the Baldridge Process lives on today at this company, as they once again won the Baldridge award in 2010. I now use the Baldridge criteria extensively in my consulting practice with my clients.

Some thoughts from my favorite singer Frank Sinatra about Never Quitting.

<u>Frank Sinatra on Never Quitting</u>
<u>on Tough Challenges: "That's Life"</u>

I've been a puppet, a pauper, a pirate, a poet, a pawn and a king…

I've been up and down, and over and out, and I know one thing…

Each time I find myself falling flat on my face, I just pick myself up and get back in the race… That's life! And I can't deny it…

Many times I've thought of quittin', but my heart just ain't gonna buy it…

MORE STORIES ABOUT ERIC FROM HIS CLASS-MATES IN GREECE

HOW ERIC GOT ME TO PICK UP A GUITAR
BY PAT CHUNG

For me, playing the guitar wasn't really about being in a band or being a rock star; it was about being able to play for my friends around a campfire. The moment, Eric found out that I had found a guitar; he immediately demanded a private show. He made me promise him to learn "Patience" by Guns and Roses. At this point, I had to wonder if there was something wrong with Eric. As I was leaving his apartment I couldn't help but ask myself how Eric could possibly think I could play Guns and Roses when I could barely tune the guitar? Whenever I wanted to just throw the guitar at the wall, I would think of Eric's excitement that first day and that ludicrous promise he made me make. Eric only really saw me play in front of people once. It was "'Anyone but You'" at my apartment at some point in February or March. I'm glad he got to see it, but I wish he were there a few months later when my dream of being a campfire rocker, the guy who got everyone to start singing came true. The song was "'Wonderwall'" by Oasis. I can't really describe what it was like when everyone in the room starting singing along. I had achieved a dream. So thanks, Eric, for everything. Thanks for bugging the hell out of me and for the kind words. Thanks for letting me achieve my dream to be the guy that inspired people to sing and brought people together. And thanks for being the guy that inspired and brought people together even without a guitar.

ERIC BEING GENUINE
BY CARRIE PETERS

I remember when Eric and I went to see an Irish band in Athens right after Spring Break. On the walk there he told me a little about his break and then turned to me and said, "So Carrie, tell me about Ireland." Eric gave me his full and sincere attention as I rambled on about seeing Castles and visiting pubs. It was exactly the right thing, I don't know how to describe it, except that having him there to listen, and knowing that he was genuinely interested it was exactly the right way to come home to Greece. So this past New Years Eve as I was listening to the pipers at a Celtic concert, I could hear Eric's voice and see him so clearly. The pipers then played "Amazing Grace," and I about lost it – but the clarity of my memory made it okay.

<u>Eric's first lesson for pursuing your Perpetual Potential™!</u>

Take on tough challenges and never quit!

What tough personal or business challenges are you facing, or should you face? How will you prepare to "Take on these tough challenges and never quit"?

LESSON NUMBER TWO: FOCUS ON WHAT YOU DO HAVE, NOT ON WHAT YOU DON'T HAVE

The first time I spoke those words to a group of people that I didn't know was the day after Eric died. Once again we were at Rosemary's house (the owner of the Athens Centre where Eric went to school in Greece). We had just seen the video that Eric's classmates made for us, and I was addressing the students. The second idea that I wanted to tell them was to focus on everything they had to be thankful for rather than focusing on having lost their friend Eric. So I told them a story about when I was helping Eric to put together his resume as he began to look for an internship and eventually a job. I remember the conversation vividly. "But, Dad," he said, "I don't have any experience. How can I possibly write a resume?"

I then began to ask Eric about some of his life experiences "But, Eric, didn't you act as lead altar boy at church from the time you were in fifth grade until you were a senior? You served as vice president of your youth group at church. You won an award for entrepreneurship at high school; also, weren't you named as the salesperson of the week at a retail job that you had; weren't you promoted to be the training person at the restaurant you worked at?"

...So you get the idea. Eric really had a lot more experience than he thought he had, and before he was finished, he had filled up a two-page resume.

I told Eric's classmates in Athens, who were all juniors and seniors in college that it would be quite easy for them to think about all the things they didn't have as they were looking for jobs and moving ahead with their lives. It would be easy for them to say things to themselves like, "I don't have enough experience; I don't have enough money; I don't have a girlfriend or a boyfriend; my car is too old; the job market is too tough...and on, and on." I told them that thinking like this would only put them in a negative spiral, and that this type of thinking would never allow them to leverage all of the skills and abilities that each of them brought to the table. In addition, that "poor me" type of thinking would never allow them to come close to achieving what their fullest potential could be.

I share this lesson with people who attend different speeches I give, specifically how I feel about all of the things I have in my life even though I lost my son: I have my beautiful wife, Marianne, who has loved me for as long as I can remember. I have my son Stephen, who is great kid—smart and funny and with unbelievable future potential. I can't wait to see how his life unfolds. I have my family, who have supported all of us in dealing with Eric's loss. I have my friends, who have stuck with me. I have my consulting clients. I have thousands of people come to hear me speak about Eric and about lessons learned from Baldrige, and now I also have all of you who are reading this book and hopefully enjoying it.

So I've chosen to focus on what I do have, not what I don't have, and I believe this has made all the difference in how I've dealt with this tragedy. This outlook has helped me to be able to look forward to how our family can continue to do good things in Eric's name.

> What will your choice be at this very moment? What are some of the skills, relationships, assets, opportunities, or options that you currently have that could be better leveraged to help you to get to the next level of your potential?

Let's take a look at a couple of things that most or all of us have that we may not think about in terms of leveraging our potential.

Eric, focusing on what he does have

RELATIONSHIPS

What direct family relationships do you have that could be stronger?

For example could you be closer to your spouse, your children, your parents, or your brothers and sisters? What would things be like in terms of the quality of your life if you invested the time and energy necessary to strengthen these relationships? If the quality of the relationships were to improve, what would this do to help you to achieve the next level of your potential? This may or may not seem obvious to you, but the more content you are in your personal relationships, the easier it will be for you to stretch yourself to try new activities, to accept the responsibilities, and to truly enjoy the challenge of completing goals and reaching new heights.

A similar question should be asked about extended family relationships, relationships with friends, and professional relationships. The old adage of "it's not only what you know; it's who you know" is true. More importantly, how strong is your relationship with those people that you know? That could make all of the difference in the pursuit of your potential.

LIFE EXPERIENCE

> Just as I questioned Eric about his life experiences in putting together his resume, it would be helpful for you to take a look at what your life experiences have been. Think about how you can leverage your experiences to take you to the next level of your potential.

I'll share just a couple of my life experiences that I'm thinking about leveraging as I'm writing this book:

1) When I was younger, music was always a very important part of my life. Not only did I like to listen to music, but I also played the trumpet from the time I was in grade school all the way through my freshman year of college. While I still listened to music through college through the time when I first got married, it became something that was kind of in the background rather than in the forefront of my life. Well one of the things I've decided to do as part of pursuing my personal potential is to make music a more important part of my life, moving forward.

So I've been out shopping for a new guitar. I've never played the guitar before, but I think I'd enjoy it as something that is for both personal relaxation and for enhancing the speeches that I make. I feel confident that I'll be successful because of my prior life experience playing the trumpet.

> Is there something that you have
> done in the past that you could
> leverage into pursuing your
> personal Perpetual Potential?

2) Something else from my past experience that I am considering to leverage is my experience in sports. I played sports all through my childhood and college years. I also coached for both of my sons as they played baseball and basketball when they were younger. Another thing that I'd like to pursue in terms of my Perpetual Potential is to get involved again in youth sports. I may become a coach once again, or I may become a referee of high school sports through a local professional organization that runs scholastic sports. So the message here is that you can use your life experience to help you achieve a higher, more sustainable use of your potential. Just because it's been a long time since you did something you loved doesn't mean you have to just think about it nostalgically. I believe that it's a huge opportunity to perpetuate your potential.

JOB EXPERIENCE

Some people know early in life what their chosen career will be. We hear stories all the time about young children saying they want to be a doctor or lawyer, a mechanic, a politician, and many other career choices, and they follow through with them. Other people go to college and find a chosen career through their studies. Then there are people like me and perhaps you are in this category too. I was a late bloomer, and it took me some time to realize the career that was best for me. In essence my career, my business, is a result of all of the jobs I experienced during my lifetime. Perhaps this describes your personal evolution as well. When I graduated from college, I first went into sales, which then led me to a career in hotel sales, which then led me to a career as a general manager in the hotel business, which then led me to opening my consulting business. I could never have imagined when I graduated from college that I would be doing what I'm doing today, consulting, speaking, and now writing. My job experiences led me to this career. So what does this mean for you?

> What job experiences have you had that
> could lead you in a new direction
> or that you could leverage into
> expanding your career today?

Could your experience working in the retail field lead to a career in sales? Could your experience in selling one type of product lead to a career selling something else? Could your experience in any field lead you to be a public speaker in that field? Could your experience in any field lead you to teach at a community college about that topic? Could your experience in the military lead you to public service? Could your experience in any field lead you to be a board member or working in some other capacity with a related nonprofit organization? Could your interest in a particular field that you have not had the opportunity to pursue lead you to going back to school to learn more about that field? Could your experience in a job that you had when you were younger lead you to go back to a similar job because you realize that you still enjoy it?

I think you can begin to see that the opportunities are really endless; all you need to do is to think about them and then to take some action. Unfortunately we tend to forget the job experiences that got us to our current career no matter how modest the job experiences might be. When you think about what you do have (these job experiences) instead of what you don't have (your dream job), it puts you on the correct pathway to finding that dream job, or at least that next job that you want.

PERSONAL KNOWLEDGE

Our personal knowledge is one thing that nobody can ever take away from us. It is always with us, and even if people take other things away, i.e. a job, money, our home, a loved one, a friend, or anything, we still have our knowledge.

> Take an inventory of all the things you learned over the years, and write it all down. What do you know or what have you learned that you can leverage into pursuing the next level of your potential?

SOMEONE ELSE'S KNOWLEDGE

Think about a teacher who might have had a profound impact on you when you were younger. Think about a friend or a peer who has achieved a level of recognition or college degree in their field. Think about a speaker that you might have heard either recently or in the past. Think about a book that you might have read that raised some interesting ideas. An example of a book that I read which raised an interesting idea that stuck with me was the book *Outliers* by Malcolm Gladwell. Gladwell presented a concept called the "ten-thousand-hour rule" where he suggested that it takes ten thousand hours of doing something to become an expert. He presented several examples of people and groups who have attained this level of expertise. This concept made me think of my own background and history in the areas about which I consult and speak. I totaled up the hours that I have been engaged in these areas, and sure enough it is well over ten thousand hours. This knowledge that I got from Mr. Gladwell has opened up my eyes into what it will take to achieve my potential in new and different future endeavors.

HELPING SOMEONE ELSE
ACHIEVE HIS OR HER DREAM

One of the best ways to put focus on what you do have is to share what you have with another person to help him or her achieve a dream. Those of us who are parents know that we do this every day with our children; it comes naturally. But what have you done to help a coworker, a friend, an employee, or a relative other than your spouse or children to help them to achieve their dreams? The first thing you have to do is to ask them what their dreams are. This requires you to really listen to them and take the focus off of yourself. Once you understand their dreams, you can then search your memory banks for the knowledge, skills, and/or expertise that you have and that you can share with them to help them to achieve their dreams.

As you share your experience and expertise, you will become acutely aware of what you do have, what you do know, what you can use to help them and to help yourself move forward.

> You see, many times "what we do have" is buried somewhere deep in our minds or our hearts. The simple act of sharing what we do have with others brings it again to the surface and allows us to leverage what we do have to perpetuate our potential.

YOUR DREAM

Does this sound at all familiar to you? "When I was younger, I always wanted to be a (fill in the blank), but (fill in the blank) happened, and I never got around to it. Oh well." I know I have many things that I could fill in the blank with: I was going to become a jazz musician. I was going to be a professional athlete. I was going to be a writer…

> What dreams have you not yet fulfilled? Do you still have some of these dreams, and are they worth pursuing? If so, what are you going to do about it?

FOCUSING ON WHAT YOU DO HAVE IN YOUR CAREER

One of the first leadership jobs I accepted was as General Manager of a mid-sized hotel. My first day on the job, I drove into the parking lot and saw a young man coming out of the kitchen with a box in his hand. He put the box in the trunk of his car, and when I approached him and looked in the box I found a stack of steaks and a couple of jugs of wine that he was stealing from the hotel. So my first official act as General Manager was to fire this kid. I found out that this was just the tip of the iceberg, and I had to fire fifty out of a hundred and fifty employees of the hotel for stealing. Instead of thinking about what I didn't have: one third of the staff needed to run the hotel, I focused on what I did have: two thirds of the employees who wanted to do the right thing. We built on this foundation, and at the end of my first year we had increased profits by 51 percent with only a 5 percent increase in sales.

I've talked about my experience in leading another company to win the Baldrige Award. What I didn't have when I started that journey was much support from the other leaders in the company or the staff. What I did have was the support of two leaders and the belief that the Baldrige process was the perfect process for this company to pursue to fulfill its potential. I built upon that foundation, and although it took a long time, converted over nine hundred employees and leaders to the same belief. The Baldrige process has played a major role in that company's success for the last fifteen years.

BACK TO DREAMS ...

Here is what I'm going to do to pursue my Perpetual Potential: When I finish writing this book, I'm going to buy a guitar and learn to play it. I'll do this both for my own enjoyment and also to enhance my public speaking business. This is currently an unfulfilled dream of mine. When this book is finished, I will have fulfilled my dream of becoming a writer. Perhaps more importantly, when I finish this book it will help Eric to achieve his dream of changing the way business is done on world markets. You see even though Eric is no longer with us physically, his Pursuit of Perpetual Potential is continuing on through Stephen, Marianne, and me.

<u>The 3 P's: Patience, Perseverance and Perseverance</u>

When things go wrong as they sometimes will,
When the road you're trudging seems all uphill,
When the funds are low, and the debts are high,
And you want to smile but have to sigh,
When care is pressing you down a bit—
Rest if you must, but do not quit.
Success is failure turned inside out,
The silver tint of the clouds of doubt,
And you can never tell how close you are.
It may be near when it seems so far.
So stick to the fight when you're hardest hit.
It's when things go wrong that you must not quit.
~ Unknown

MORE STORIES ABOUT
ERIC FROM HIS FRIENDS:

TRANSITIONS
BY AMANDA BRAATZ

One conversation I had with him that will always stay with me is one that we had one night while we were on our trip to the Argolid in Nauplion. We started talking about how we both chose to come to Greece. We both felt that we already had undergone some changes while in Greece. I said that I had had issues with shyness and insecurity in the past and was trying to break free of those, first at college and now in Athens. Eric said that he felt like for the first time in his life he was truly able to be himself. He said that there were few people, namely his family and best friends, who knew the real Eric. I think he was meaning to say that he was getting a clearer picture of himself while in Greece and maybe thought he had been missing that in other parts of his life. He told me that for knowing us for such a short period of time, he already felt extremely comfortable around all of us and didn't feel the need to act like anything but himself and that he intended to go home continuing to do just that. I'm so glad Eric shared this with me, especially looking back on it now. I'm glad that in some way Greece and we, his friends, were able to give him the final pushes he needed to be at peace with who he was and how he wanted to be in his life.

HERE COMES THE SUN
BY CHRISTOPHER MASON (ERIC AND
STEPHEN'S COUSIN)

With his jet-black hair and clean white skin my cousin Eric could easily pass for a member of The Beatles. Standing 6'4" and wearing a size fourteen dress shoe with his light brown leather jacket and a pressed dress shirt with a tie, this image sticks out in my mind when I remember my cousin. Eric had a very strong faith and showed this by serving in the church altar, going to church every Sunday, singing in the choir, and dancing in our Greek dancing group. Eric and Stephen really opened my eyes to my church and being with them and going to my church made my faith stronger. I can say that Eric strengthened my faith. I always wanted to be like my cousins. I looked up to Stephen, and Stephen and I both looked up to Eric. I remember I wanted to be like Eric when I saw him and Steve serving at the altar. When I was seven I was put in Eric and Stephen's group. Eric was the captain and was in charge of everyone. Once again he showed me what to do and taught me the ropes. He was always so cool and collected. My theo (uncle) Bob, he told us one way that we could keep him in our life. "Take Eric's strong positive traits and implement them in your everyday life." I do just that. The last words in "Here Comes the Sun" are "it's alright." It is all right, because someday I will see my cousin again. Until then, I hope that he is having a good time and playing basketball in heaven.

***Eric Greek Dancing with Phillip, friend
and Taverna owner—Here comes the Sun!***

<u>Eric's Second Lesson for Pursuing</u>
<u>Your Perpetual Potential</u> ™!
Focus on what you do have, not on what you don't have.

This is perhaps the best piece of advice I gave to myself in coping with Eric's death. I feel this concept is both simple and elegant. If you're not sure of everything that you do have, ask someone close to you to help you take an inventory and then think about how you can leverage everything you do have. I bet it is more than you think!

Lesson Number Three: Change the Stars

The last time I spoke to Eric was about one week before a reckless driver ran onto the sidewalk and hit him. During this conversation several interesting things occurred. The first thing I remember is that I heard music, pretty loud music, playing in the background behind Eric's voice. I asked him to turn the radio down so I could hear him better, and he chuckled when I said that. "Dad, that is not a radio; that's a man in front of our apartment playing the accordion." I chuckled too and asked Eric who the man was that was playing the accordion. Eric told me that this gentleman lived in the neighborhood and very routinely walked around serenading his neighbors. When Marianne and I went to Athens, Katja took us to see Eric's apartment building. Sure enough the man with the accordion was accompanying us as we walked.

The next difference that I remember from previous conversations with Eric was that he seemed extremely calm and mellow, even more so than usual. He started to tell me something that quite honestly really tickled me. He said, "Dad, I finally understand it." Of course I asked him what he was talking about, and he continued, "I finally understand that I can do anything that I want to do and be anything that I want to be." Eric couldn't see me but my mouth dropped wide open for just a moment and then a big smile came onto my face.

You see, this was one of the life lessons that I always stressed to both Eric and Stephen. The only limitation on what a person can be or what they can do with their life is really in their own minds. Our city, our state, our country, our world, and our universe all offer so many wonderful opportunities to all of us. It really is up to us to figure out a way to take advantage of and enjoy these opportunities.

Eric's four-thousand-mile journey had paid off. At the other end of the world over the telephone from Athens, Greece, my son Eric was telling me that he had finally figured it out. I was thrilled for him! My next question was of course, "How did you finally figure this out?" His answer shed a lot of light for me on why this trip to Athens was so important to Eric and the true value that this trip held for him. The true value was not in the credits that he received for his studies. It was not in the beautiful sights that he was able to witness during his three months in Greece. The true value of this trip for Eric was that it gave him time to evaluate his life and determine what direction he wanted to take. Amanda's thoughts, shared with you earlier, ring true as I reflect on my phone conversation with Eric.

Eric sounded so peaceful during that phone conversation that I chose not to mention something to him that I had "bugged" him about in every conversation prior to this. I always was asking him what his plans were for finding a summer internship when he came back from Greece. It just didn't feel right to ask him or to bother him with that trivial detail after the revelation he had come to, and the peaceful state of mind he had achieved. I'm so glad I didn't ask him. I want to fast forward from that conversation now to my last day in Athens after Eric had died.

Marianne had gone home the previous day to make arrangements for the funeral, and I was waiting to make sure that there were no additional difficulties in having Eric's body released to come back home. It was around midnight, I packed all of my clothes and was looking at Eric's suitcase which I was going to be bringing home, when I decided to open the suitcase and just take a look through Eric's belongings. I came upon his portfolio and inside I found the three poems. For some reason I'd never seen any of the poems that he wrote, and yet there they were. I don't understand why he had those poems with him in Greece, so I can only chalk it up to be another one of those spiritual happenings that I talked about earlier. I lingered over the third one, titled "Stars," which I'd like to share with you:

STARS

Some say destiny calls
to us,   yanking on the chains of hereditary
bondage. Though not unbearable,
they are challenging to re-forge.

But how does one discover the chains?

They are neither real,   nor imaginary, yet
still hold us down: tying us to what we must become.

Bitter acceptance… Silent ignorance… Vengeful denial…

   … And yet…

…*the chains still remain…*

But some,   some still fight,   unable
to accept,   unable to deny,   unable
to ignore…   *Why?* God's greatest gift to man…..

HOPE.   At the end of the day,   perhaps,

   A man can change the stars.

                              Eric Michael Stearns

I read the poem about half a dozen times with such pride. How could these words come from a fifteen-year-old boy? Of course I immediately knew the answer, or I thought I did. There was a second page attached to the poem. Apparently Eric's teacher had asked the students to explain the rationale behind the poems they had written in class. Following are Eric's words about the meaning behind the poem:

"This is the first poem I've ever written, yet I try to do the same thing I do in my stories. Spark thought into the reader's mind. Whether you believe in destiny or not, you are still bound by some unforeseen thing. You aren't able to break it, but you can change it to your whim. My dad always told me I can be anything I wish to be; that is where this thought sparked up from. The idea of the poem came at the very end, when I wrote the last line. I always have found it rather calm and tranquil to just stare up into the stars, which are so beautiful yet always out of reach. I have always strived for the stars, growing up as someone who has had to win or be the best with the absence of failure. I will always strive to be the best, but I will also continue working to get that need to be the best out of my system."

I told you earlier that Eric was a deep thinker. Eric was a writer, and one of the things he was struggling with was whether he could continue his writing and also pursue a career in business. After reading his poem and rationale I realized how long Eric had been thinking about this idea of being able to be anything that he wanted to be. I was so happy that he had resolved it for himself while he was in Greece.

> Understanding that he could be anything that he wanted to be set Eric's spirit free—there is no better, more liberating feeling that a man can experience!

So how does this concept of "Changing the Stars" apply to each of us? Let's examine some of the words from Eric's poem.

> *Some say destiny calls to us, yanking on*
> *the chains of hereditary bondage.*
> *But how does one discover the chains? They are neither*
> *real, nor imaginary, yet still hold us down: tying us to*
> *what we must become.*

How did you discover what your destiny was? Did someone tell you what you should do with your life or tell you what you would never be able to do with your life? Did you tell yourself that you'd never be able to do something? The chains that we sometimes feel are between real and imaginary, in other words there is typically some truth to the chains that keep us from doing the things that we want to do, or that we have the potential to do. The imaginary chains that we have concocted in our minds are things we tell ourselves that we can't do; we have more control over breaking these chains than we believe. However if we don't address the imaginary chains we will never be able to break the real chains.

> *But some, some still fight, unable to accept,*
> *unable to deny, unable to ignore…*
> *Why? God's greatest gift to man… HOPE.*
> *At the end of the day, perhaps*
> *A man can change the stars.*

CHANGING THE STARS IN BUSINESS

I want to share with you a story of a friend and client of mine. He had taken a new, very responsible job and was asked to increase the sales and profits for his division. However, he wasn't given the resources that he needed to achieve these goals. He was trying to do the best he could but was making very little progress. I talked with him and flat out told him that I thought he was "in a box" and that if he didn't do something bold and breakthrough, he would become very frustrated, would not hit his goals, and in the process would alienate his people. He got very angry with me when I said this, but I felt that as his friend I owed it to him to tell him the truth as I saw it. He got so angry that he wouldn't talk to me for about six months.

I felt awful about the prospect of losing this friend, but I felt worse about letting him try to fight the imaginary chains that were binding him. Sure enough, in a very short time he not only broke the chains, but also accomplished the major acquisition of a new business that will benefit his company for a long time to come. My friend had indeed "changed the stars" for his company and himself. I am very proud of him!

I've shared with you how I changed the stars at one company where I worked, and I'd like to tell you more about that experience. I started out with three people out of nine hundred being interested in pursuing Baldrige and eventually got even the strongest doubters on board with the initiative. I dramatically changed the culture at this company, one person at a time. This was accomplished through many one-on-one conversations with key people in the company. I also invited people in from companies who had won the Baldrige to speak to our management team about their company's experiences and the benefits they had reaped from their Baldrige journey.

Perhaps the most effective mechanism I used was something called the President's Quality Review. In essence I conducted mini-Baldrige assessments with every individual department in the company, and thus personally immersed almost 90 percent of the employees in the Baldrige journey. They could see the results for themselves, a critical mass of Baldrige "disciples" had been created, and Providence moved! The Baldrige Award was just around the corner.

<u>Eric's Third lesson for pursuing
your Perpetual Potential</u>™!

So how, exactly do you change the stars?

One star at a time… Once you evolve a
critical mass of stars, Providence moves!
You will begin to see the changes you
desire in yourself and in others.

One way Eric changed the stars was to have
a positive impact on everyone he knew.
Which stars do you want to change, and
how are you preparing to do so?

THE ERIC MICHAEL STEARNS "CHANGE THE STARS" SCHOLARSHIP

In January of 2009 we held a memorial service at Penn State so that Eric's friends and classmates who couldn't attend his funeral could get some closure. Dr. Jim Thomas, the Dean of Smeal Business College at the University; Dina Guthoff, Eric's academic advisor; and Jerry Benito, the Programs Coordinator at Smeal, worked tirelessly to make this event happen. Their kindness is a debt I can never fully repay. I want to share with you a portion of what Dina had to say about Eric to more than one hundred students who attended this service:

"From the first day I met Eric, his goal was to study abroad in Greece. With over four hundred students in my caseload, it is sometimes difficult to really get to know all of them. Eric was one of those special freshman students that really stood out to me. He was enthusiastic about everything he did, most uniquely about seeing the country of his heritage, searching his ancestry, and immersing himself in the culture. I saw him the day before he went home for winter break, and he was almost unable to contain his enthusiasm of leaving for Greece about three weeks from then.

"I received a brief email from him when he arrived in Athens. He wanted me to know that he had made it there safely, had already met so many wonderful people, and was in love with the country. The day before his accident I received my final email from Eric which he ended, 'I want you to know my time in Greece has been amazing. It has been a life altering experience and one I will never forget.' A few days later, he was gone.

"Eric was always concerned about leaving his mark on the world, and we had many discussions about that. As a parent it amazed me that Eric could not see that his mere existence in this world was already leaving a mark on all those who came in contact with him. He was a happy young man, with great values and standards, and a wonderful spirit. Eric will never be forgotten, and his mark will forever be on my heart. Any time I hear about Greece, anytime I see baklava, anytime I pass by our International Programs Reading Lounge and see his collage of photos, he will be forever present. Eric always appreciated the time I spent with him. But the truth is that I had the great honor to have known someone as special as Eric."

Eric is still achieving his life's goal and fulfilling his Perpetual Potential through others as witnessed by this excerpt from a letter written by one of the recipients of the Eric Michael Stearns "Change the Stars" scholarship at Penn State University:

"I've been looking forward to my study abroad experience almost as long as I can remember. As I began my research to write this letter, I spoke with two of the many individuals who knew Eric personally...I was struck by what a truly exceptional and special individual Eric was—their descriptions of his upbeat nature, thoughtful disposition, and love for knowledge were evoked lovingly and not without emotion. Like Eric, I am extremely interested in the interplay of international markets, specifically in the Latin American region. In receiving this scholarship, I hope to honor Eric's heartfelt nature, love of culture, and passion for life. One of Eric's study abroad mates mentioned to me via email 'We haven't forgotten him.' After learning about Eric and his beautiful life, I can affirm that his remarkable story will remain with me throughout out my study abroad semester, and beyond."

<u>Eric's life goal was to change the way business is done on world markets</u>.

He wanted to influence other people's lives for the better, to Change the Stars.

In the current world marketplace, Senior Leaders make most decisions and the bulk of employees are locked into minor roles. Eric dreamed of business models, like Baldrige, that would allow every employee to have international impact by being personally invested in the company's customers, culture and products.

Eric's "Change the Stars" scholarship will allow him to achieve that dream through the actions and deeds of the scholarship recipients in their future companies.

Epilogue

I hope that by reading this book you've picked up a few ideas of how you can change the stars in your own world. There are a multitude of stars. The change could be in your business, a humanitarian cause, a hobby, your education, helping someone else, or working towards your personal potential.

Stephen has accepted Eric's challenge to "change the stars" by completing an internship last summer, completing College, and accepting his first job. Stephen's potential is unlimited!

Marianne has accepted Eric's challenge to "change the stars" by becoming a role model for and helping others who have to deal with a tragedy, by leading her church out of dark times, and by accepting a leadership role in the community.

I have accepted Eric's challenge to "change the stars" by writing this book, by speaking about Eric to business and college audiences, and by continually renewing my spark to perpetually pursue my potential and to help others pursue theirs.

Eric's existence and the way he treated people had an impact on everyone he touched, and he is still having an impact today. He is still pursuing his Perpetual Potential through everyone who knew him. Now this includes you.

Eric's challenge to you and me: "Change the Stars, baby... Change the Stars!

A CLOSING MESSAGE FROM BOB:

Thank you for taking the time to get to know Eric and to learn about the amazing legacy he left to us. If you would like more information about Eric, about Perpetual Potential, or about the three lessons described in the book, please contact me at (724) 933-3935 or bobstearns@extraordinary-performance.com.

11539452R00051

Made in the USA
Charleston, SC
04 March 2012